NASCAR RACING

Tony Stewart

by Kristal Leebrick

Consultant:
Betty L. Carlan
Research Librarian
International Motorsports Hall of Fame
Talladega, Alabama

Capstone press

Mankato, Minnesota

Edge Books are published by Capstone Press
151 Good Counsel Drive, P.O. Box 669, Mankato, Minnesota 56002
www.capstonepress.com

Library of Congress Cataloging-in-Publication Data
Leebrick, Kristal, 1958–
    Tony Stewart / by Kristal Leebrick.
        p. cm.—(Edge Books. NASCAR racing)
    Summary: Traces the life and career of Tony Stewart from his early years racing
go-karts to his titles in Indy car and stock car racing.
    Includes bibliographical references and index.
    ISBN 0-7368-2425-1 (hardcover)
    1. Stewart, Tony, 1971– —Juvenile literature. 2. Automobile racing drivers—
United States—Biography—Juvenile literature. 3. NASCAR (Association)—Juvenile
literature. [1. Stewart, Tony, 1971– 2. Automobile racing drivers.] I. Title. II. Series.
GV1032.S743L44 2004
796.72'092—dc22   2003014783

(handwritten) 650 3573

Editorial Credits
Matt Doeden, editor; Jason Knudson, designer; Jo Miller, photo researcher

Photo Credits
Artemis Images/Indianapolis Motor Speedway, 17; Inside Racing/Andy Clark, 13, 20;
    Inside Racing/Randy Jones, 11; True Speed Enterprises, 8
Getty Images/Chris Stanford, 28; David Taylor, 15, 21; Jonathan Ferrey, 5, 7;
    Matthew Stockman, 19; Robert Laberge, 25
SportsChrome-USA/Brian Spurlock, 23; Greg Crisp, cover (portrait), cover (car)

1 2 3 4 5 6 09 08 07 06 05 04

Table of Contents

CHAPTER 1

NASCAR Champion

Tony Stewart and 42 other NASCAR drivers slowly circled Richmond International Raceway on May 5, 2002. As a NASCAR official waved a green flag, all 43 drivers stomped on their gas pedals.

Tony liked racing at Richmond. He had already won there twice in his career. But he had not done well so far in the 2002 season. He ranked 10th in the driver standings. He needed a win to pull closer to the leaders.

Tony started the race in the 41st position. His team had changed the car's engine after he had qualified third for the race. NASCAR rules make teams that change engines start at the back of the field.

Tony (#20) raced Ryan Newman (#12) for the lead at Richmond International Raceway.

Learn about:

→ Tony's 2002 championship

→ Tony's childhood

→ Tony's early racing career

Early in the race, Tony was not happy with his car. It did not handle the way he wanted. He kept working, though. Good driving and good pit strategy slowly moved Tony toward the front. The team continued to adjust the car during pit stops. Tony kept passing other drivers.

With 28 laps to go, Tony trailed only Ryan Newman. Tony then made a move inside to take the lead. For the next several laps, Newman followed closely on Tony's bumper. But Newman could not get around him.

With 22 laps remaining, Dave Blaney's engine blew up. The pace car came onto the track as a caution flag flew. Four laps later, the racing started again. Tony timed the restart perfectly. He pulled more than three car lengths ahead of Newman. Newman could not catch up. Tony won the race.

"I was down after the first 50 laps. But the guys kept digging and I couldn't give up on them . . . I never would have dreamed we could have got up here today."
—Tony Stewart, *The Augusta Chronicle*, 5-5-02

Tony's win at Richmond moved him up to eighth in the standings. As the season went on, Tony continued to climb in the standings. He earned his first Winston Cup title in the last race of the season.

Tony spun his tires to celebrate his Richmond win.

The Early Years

Tony Stewart was born May 20, 1971. He grew up in Columbus, Indiana, with his parents, Nelson and Pam, and his younger sister, Natalie. He attended Columbus North High School, where he played trombone in the school band. He also spent time playing basketball and hanging out with friends.

Tony wanted to be a race car driver at a young age.

Tony wanted to be a race car driver from a young age. When Tony was 5, Nelson bought him a go-kart. At 7, Tony began taking part in organized races.

Five years later, Tony entered the International Karting Federation Grand National Championship. This event is the biggest race in the sport. Tony won the race, beating older and more experienced drivers.

By the time Tony was 15, his behavior was becoming a problem. He often refused to do his chores. One day, Nelson told Tony to mow the lawn. Tony did not do it. Nelson was angry. He punished Tony by selling the go-kart.

"Seeing that kart disappear down the street absolutely destroyed me. I finished mowing the yard, but I was literally crying my eyes out the whole time."
—Tony Stewart, *True Speed: My Racing Life*, 2002

CHAPTER 2

Small Tracks to the Big Time

Two weeks after Nelson sold Tony's go-kart, a man named Don Williams asked Tony to drive his enduro kart. These go-karts can go more than 100 miles (160 kilometers) per hour. They race on large road courses at famous tracks around the United States.

Tony raced enduro karts for two years with the World Karting Association (WKA). His first race was at Daytona International Speedway in Florida. In 1987, he won the WKA national title.

Tony raced minicars along with many other types of vehicles.

Learn about:

→ The Triple Crown

→ Tony's first NASCAR deal

→ Racing Indy cars

Winning at All Levels

In 1989, Tony began racing three-quarter (TQ) midget cars. Many young drivers practice their racing skills in these small cars. TQ midgets are expensive. Tony's family could not afford to buy one. They met Roy Barker, who had a car but needed money to get it ready for the track. Nelson gave Barker $500 to prepare the car. Barker agreed to let Tony drive it.

Two years later, Tony joined the U.S. Auto Club (USAC) and won the 1991 Rookie of the Year Award. In 1994, he won the USAC's National Midget championship. In 1995, he won the Triple Crown by winning the National Midget, Sprint, and Silver Crown titles. No other driver has won all three titles in the same year.

Tony drove every kind of race car he could.

Bigger Races

The racing world quickly noticed Tony's skill. In 1995, stock car owner Lorin Ranier asked Tony to drive a car in NASCAR's Busch Series. Tony had not thought much about stock car racing. He wanted to race Indy cars, but he could not pass up the chance. He tried to qualify for the last Busch Series race of the season, but a crash kept him out of the race.

In 1996, the Indy Racing League (IRL) formed. Racing legend A. J. Foyt asked Tony to drive his car in the league. It was Tony's dream to race Indy cars for one of his heroes. But Foyt did not want to share Tony with a stock car team. Tony had already promised Ranier that he would race in the Busch Series. Tony had to say no to Foyt.

Later, John Menard asked Tony to test one of his Indy cars. Tony performed so well that Menard decided to build a team for him. He agreed to let Tony also continue driving in the Busch Series. Tony's dream of driving an Indy car had finally come true.

Tony qualified eighth for his first IRL race. At first, he drove carefully and held his position. Later, he began to catch the leaders. After 28 laps, he led the race. He fought for the lead all day. But near the end of the race, he brushed the wall. He finished second.

Tony drove the Menards car in the IRL.

CHAPTER 3

Double Duty

In 1996, Tony drove both Indy cars and stock cars. He also drove midgets, sprint cars, and almost anything else he could race.

Tony was just learning how to drive a stock car. He often struggled during races. He had a hard time handling a stock car, which is much bigger than an Indy car. Tony did not even qualify for some of the Busch Series races.

Tony quickly became a star in the IRL.

Learn about:

→ Stock car struggles

→ A terrible crash

→ Tony's IRL championship

IRL Struggles

In May, Tony qualified for the Indianapolis 500, the world's most famous race. On one of the qualifying test laps, he averaged more than 237 miles (381 kilometers) per hour. It was the fastest timed lap in the track's history.

Tony entered the race excited about his chances to win. He led the first 32 laps of the race. But his engine blew up on lap 81. He finished 24th.

Later in 1996, Tony crashed in the last race of the IRL season. His right rear tire blew out and sent him spinning into the wall. He broke several bones. He did not drive again that year.

"My entire left side was beaten up. I had a broken collarbone, a fractured pelvis, a fractured hip, and a cracked scapula. I hadn't ever felt that kind of pain in my life."

—Tony Stewart, *True Speed: My Racing Life*, 2002

Tony (bottom right) started the 1996 Indianapolis 500 from the pole.

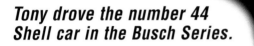

**Tony drove the number 44
Shell car in the Busch Series.**

IRL Champion

Tony joined Joe Gibbs' stock car team in 1997. He drove in five Busch Series races for Gibbs that season. He drove in 22 more races for Gibbs in 1998.

Tony spent most of 1997 racing his Indy car. In May, he qualified second for the Indianapolis 500. He brushed the wall late in the race and finished fifth.

Tony continued to finish well in his IRL races. He won his first IRL race at Pikes Peak International Raceway in Colorado. At the season's end, he led the league in points. He was the IRL champion.

Tony tried to repeat as champion in 1998. The season started well for him. He led the IRL standings after five races. But he struggled late in the season and finished third.

1998 was Tony's last full season in the IRL.

CHAPTER 4

NASCAR Star

Tony left his IRL team in 1999 to join NASCAR's Winston Cup Series. He was a success right away. He won three races during his rookie year. His first win came September 11 in Richmond. He finished fourth in the series standings and was named Rookie of the Year.

Tony also took part in the Indianapolis 500 in 1999. Tony finished ninth. He then flew to Charlotte, North Carolina, for NASCAR's Coca-Cola 600. He finished fourth. Tony had driven almost 1,100 miles (1,770 kilometers) in one day. Tony drove in both races again in 2001.

Tony joined NASCAR's Winston Cup Series in 1999.

Learn about:

→ Tony's rookie season

→ A Daytona crash

→ Temper troubles

Battling for the Cup

Many racing experts thought Tony could win the Winston Cup title in 2000. Tony won six races that year, more than any other driver. He also had many bad finishes. He finished sixth in the standings.

Tony started the 2001 season badly. In the Daytona 500, he was involved in a big crash late in the race. Tony was running fifth when the crash began. His car flew into the air and flipped several times. The car landed on top of Bobby Labonte's car. Both drivers were all right. Later in the race, NASCAR legend Dale Earnhardt was killed in another crash.

Tony's 2001 season improved after Daytona. He won three races and finished second to Jeff Gordon in the series standings.

In 2002, Tony again started the season poorly. His engine blew up during the first lap of the Daytona 500. He finished last in the biggest race of the season.

After Daytona, Tony's luck changed. He won three races during the season and had few poor finishes. In the last race of the season, he needed to finish 22nd or better to beat Mark Martin for the championship. Tony finished 18th. He was the Winston Cup champion.

Tony's car flipped in the air late in the 2001 Daytona 500.

Off the Track

Tony's temper gets him in trouble on and off the track. In 2001, he slammed into Jeff Gordon's car after a race. That year, he also kicked a reporter's tape recorder under a truck and shoved a NASCAR official. In 2002, Tony tried to kick a photographer after a race. NASCAR officials asked Tony to go to anger management classes. The classes taught Tony to control his temper.

Tony spends most of his free time around racetracks. He enjoys racing at small dirt tracks around the United States. He likes to reward racing fans who attend local tracks every week. Tony also owns several sprint cars in the World of Outlaws Series. Tony says owning the cars allows him to give something back to the racing world and its fans.

"I'm not ashamed to say I've got a problem controlling my temper, and I'm looking forward to getting with someone that can help me control that. It will make my life a lot happier."
—Tony Stewart, *AP*, 9-7-02

Career Statistics

Tony Stewart

Year	Starts	Wins	Top-5s	Top-10s	Winnings
Indy Racing League					
1996	5	0	1	1	$422,303
1997	8	1	4	6	$1,017,450
1998	11	2	5	6	$1,002,850
Career*	24	3	10	15	$2,848,123

*Career IRL statistics include finishes from 1999 and 2001 Indianapolis 500

Year	Starts	Wins	Top-5s	Top-10s	Winnings
NASCAR Winston Cup					
1999	34	3	12	20	$2,451,939
2000	34	6	12	15	$3,093,685
2001	36	3	15	22	$3,180,391
2002	36	3	15	21	$4,437,098
2003**	29	1	8	12	$4,101,560
Career	169	16	62	90	$17,264,673

**2003 statistics through 10-1-03

Career Highlights

1976   Tony's dad buys him his first go-kart.

1987   Tony wins the World Karting Association national title.

1991   Tony is named the U.S. Auto Club's Rookie of the Year.

1994   Tony wins the USAC's National Midget title.

1995   Tony becomes the only driver to win the USAC Triple Crown.

1997   Tony wins the Indy Racing League championship; he also joins the Joe Gibbs NASCAR team and races in the Busch Series.

1999   Tony is named Winston Cup's Rookie of the Year and finishes fourth in points; he makes history by driving in two races in one day: the Indianapolis 500 and a Coca-Cola 600.

2000   Tony wins six Winston Cup races, more than any other driver.

2001   Tony wins three races and finishes second to Jeff Gordon in the Winston Cup standings.

2002   Tony recovers from a Daytona 500 crash to Winston Cup title.

2003   Tony starts his 150th Winston Cup race

Glossary

caution (KAW-shun)—a period during a race when, for safety reasons, drivers cannot pass one another on the track

midget (MIJ-it)—a small race car that runs mainly on small oval tracks and dirt tracks

qualify (KWAHL-uh-fye)—to earn a starting spot in a race by completing timed laps

rookie (RUK-ee)—a first-year driver

series (SIHR-eez)—a group of races that makes up one season; drivers earn points for finishing races in a series.

win the

Read More

Bisson, Terry. *Tradin' Paint: Raceway Rookies and Royalty.* New York: Scholastic, 2001.

Johnstone, Michael. *NASCAR.* The Need for Speed. Minneapolis: LernerSports, 2002.

Teitelbaum, Michael. *Tony Stewart, Instant Superstar!* World of NASCAR. Excelsior, Minn.: Tradition Books, 2003.

Useful Addresses

Indianapolis Motor Speedway
4790 West 16th Street
Indianapolis, IN 46222

International Motorsports Hall of Fame
P.O. Box 1018
Talladega, AL 35161

NASCAR
P.O. Box 2875
Daytona Beach, FL 32120

Internet Sites

FactHound offers a safe, fun way to find Internet sites related to this book. All of the sites on FactHound have been researched by our staff.

Here's how:

1. Visit *www.facthound.com*
2. Type in this special code **0736824251** for age-appropriate sites. Or enter a search word related to this book for a more general search.
3. Click on the **Fetch It** button.

FactHound will fetch the best sites for you!

Index

31

Career Highlights

1976   Tony's dad buys him his first go-kart.

1987   Tony wins the World Karting Association national title.

1991   Tony is named the U.S. Auto Club's Rookie of the Year.

1994   Tony wins the USAC's National Midget title.

1995   Tony becomes the only driver to win the USAC Triple Crown.

1997   Tony wins the Indy Racing League championship; he also joins the Joe Gibbs NASCAR team and races in the Busch Series.

1999   Tony is named Winston Cup's Rookie of the Year and finishes fourth in points; he makes history by driving in two races in one day: the Indianapolis 500 and a Coca-Cola 600.

2000   Tony wins six Winston Cup races, more than any other driver.

2001   Tony wins three races and finishes second to Jeff Gordon in the Winston Cup standings.

2002   Tony recovers from a Daytona 500 crash to win the Winston Cup title.

2003   Tony starts his 150th Winston Cup race.

Glossary

caution (KAW-shun)—a period during a race when, for safety reasons, drivers cannot pass one another on the track

midget (MIJ-it)—a small race car that runs mainly on small oval tracks and dirt tracks

qualify (KWAHL-uh-fye)—to earn a starting spot in a race by completing timed laps

rookie (RUK-ee)—a first-year driver

series (SIHR-eez)—a group of races that makes up one season; drivers earn points for finishing races in a series.

Read More

Bisson, Terry. *Tradin' Paint: Raceway Rookies and Royalty.* New York: Scholastic, 2001.

Johnstone, Michael. *NASCAR.* The Need for Speed. Minneapolis: LernerSports, 2002.

Teitelbaum, Michael. *Tony Stewart, Instant Superstar!* World of NASCAR. Excelsior, Minn.: Tradition Books, 2003.

Useful Addresses

Indianapolis Motor Speedway
4790 West 16th Street
Indianapolis, IN 46222

International Motorsports Hall of Fame
P.O. Box 1018
Talladega, AL 35161

NASCAR
P.O. Box 2875
Daytona Beach, FL 32120

Internet Sites

FactHound offers a safe, fun way to find Internet sites related to this book. All of the sites on FactHound have been researched by our staff.

Here's how:

1. Visit *www.facthound.com*
2. Type in this special code **0736824251** for age-appropriate sites. Or enter a search word related to this book for a more general search.
3. Click on the **Fetch It** button.

FactHound will fetch the best sites for you!

Index